Mixed Blessings

A Compendium of Thoughts on Life

Ru Otto

Copyright©2016 by Ru Otto
ALL RIGHTS RESERVED
PRINTED IN THE UNITED STATES OF AMERICA
FIRST EDITION: November 2016

Table of Contents

Chapter 1: *Animal Magnetism*

Jay	3
Leda's Swan Song	4
Thanksgiving	6
Goodbye Mr. Goldenbirch	7
Song Bird	10
Breaking Ice at Dawn	11
October Rains	12
Cats Fly A Sign	15

Chapter 2: *Singing the Blues*

White Heat	18
Timekeeper	20
Ain't Nothin' Free	21
Flood Time	22
Oil Spill Tar Babies	23
Friendless at Christmas	24
Mercy Fuck	25
Food Stamp Blues	26
Calendar Notes	27

Chapter 3: *Family Affair*

Birthright	29
Moving Day	32
Fort Defiance – A Day at the Park	33
House of Glass	36
Sailing	38
Family Line	39

Chapter 4: *Matters of the Heart*

Come Close My Love	42
Mirroring Phenomena	43
High Tide	44
Please Baby Come	46

Orange is the Moon	47
Nectar Eater	48
Another Autumn	49
Taurus Moon	50
Over Soul Love Song	52
Mercy	54
Passing the Night	56

Chapter 5: *Summation*

And Later	59
The Nature of My Reality	60
Conversations with Trees	62
The Wisdom of Crows	67
Fare Thee Well	68
Journey's End	69
Reflections	70
Body of Work	71
The Need for Renewal	72

Chapter 1
Animal Magnetism

Jay – Behemoth at the Feeder

Raucous streak of indigo

Winged cacophony,

Clumsy crashing against the feeder,

Seeds flying everywhere,

While screech and squawk

Fill damp air.

Has he landed

Or just swooped low,

And fallen there?

Cocksure he looks about,

Black crest twitching his cranky pleasure.

Leda's Swan Song

Some days a trick of fate

Or the gods in a fit of fancy

Beget a match of unfathomable complexity

Understandable only to themselves.

The outer world rejects the coupling

And upon shallow reflection

So do I.

But as you slowly glide into my waiting arms

Your body iridescent with untamed beauty,

I forget the rules

The taboos of my so-called civilization

Fall away from me,

They fade like a fevered dream

And I am transfixed

By the white gossamer of your curving neck

Caressing whisper-soft against my cheek,

And who could deny the glory of a moment filled

With dazzling wings

Opalescent fans unfurling above and around me

Blocking out the sun and enfolding me

In an exaltation of desire.

Later, I lay enraptured

Face buried in your downy breast

Unmindful and oblivious of everything

But a deeper current of truth,

And the comfort of knowing and loving

A kindred spirit.

Thanksgiving: The Carcass and I

Cooked that bird and ate it alone

Sweet meat slipping right out' them bones

Carcass slid open

Slick as you please,

No regrets

No reprieves

Goodbye Mr. Goldenbirch

My neighbors said that old white dog
Was like a husband to Ethel Goldenbirch.
He kept watch
Coffee brown eyes alert with tears,
Tarry salt tracks staining
The snowy scruff of his muzzle,
While she moaned through the night,
Sugar burning through capillary and nerve,
Her vision growing dim,
Time and diabetes
Loosening her otherwise
Tenacious grasp on life.

She never made it to the last inevitable
Countermeasure of this disease.
No sharp needle ever sank insulin
Into her wasted thigh.
When she died,
Her heart just stopped,
Became silent as the center of a hurricane.

Left me at a loss.
What to do with this huge, filthy animal
That no one wanted.
Weeks on end he mourned her passing,
Hiding out of sight under my house,
Continuing to keep watch, thinking his thoughts,
And digging holes to bury himself
With soft Florida sand.

I missed her too,
And sometimes grief can create
An openhearted space.
Soon his sad face pried open my heart,
And my screen door.
I gave him a bath and let him in.
I let him ALL the way in.
The next five years were filled
With his unquestioning devotion to me
And the mingling of a surprising humor
That flowed between us.
I swear, we laughed together
At his droll silliness

And found comfort

In our shared memories of her,

My best friend,

His only companion.

And so, when his time came

He went down real easy,

Went back to being her old man,

Slipped off to sleep

And followed her in his dreams,

As his needled arm relaxed,

Stretching down the long metal length

Of the veterinarian's table

And surely, finally,

In the now empty cabin they once shared

Nestled deep in the warm Florida night,

A dusty window reflects the light

Of two stars

Now joined,

And disappearing from sight

Song Bird

A note,
High and sweet,
Breaks free of the crowd,
Soars over the muddle.
Pure spirit released,
In joy
And gratitude.
Cold glances of surprise
Cannot dim my rapture.

Breaking Ice at Dawn

Slipping from warm bed into January dawn,
Well-padded and clumsy with down,
Melting the brittle air in a world of cold silences,
Softened only by huff of horse breath
There, near my left shoulder
And behind my swaddled head.
He stands, expectant, beloved, waits
For my pick-ax to fall, patient
For this morning gift of water soaking
Through the splintering ice.
Massive head on graceful neck
Lowered now to drink, accepts
The daily offering of my labor.
Tiny shards of ice catch fire in the light,
Airborne crystals sparkle like jewels,
Stick to my coat and skitter across the frozen pond.
I swing the ax in rhythm with my heart
As my arm arches with the rising sun.

October Rains

I like to fall asleep to the rain in October.

The windswept raindrops pelt my windows and roof

They sooth me and I sleep hard

I sleep

Like a winter bear dreaming-in the great migration of salmon.

Those gape-mouthed behemoths who circle and wait in the fringes of our rocky coast

For just this moment of autumn deluge,

Memory and sex driving them relentlessly

To search the flooding streambeds,

Nosing for the scent of home and safety.

For lodged in each reptilian brain lies an instinctual map to their spawning grounds,

The perfect place to drop their chromosomal package

And hurl themselves into the future.

King of Fish, benevolent gift of providence,

They fling themselves forward,

Plunging upstream,

Scraped and bruised by rock and gravel,

Until, in a final act of piscine ecstasy,

Expelling sperm and eggs over rock studded runnels,

And gasping,

They die in droves,

Covering the streambeds for miles with the stench

Of life and death.

And so, growling and frisking,

The bears feast with coyote and wolves, eagle and crow

Every living creature sharing in this bounty of flesh

Sharp teeth crunch bone,

Tongues loll in loose lipped pleasure,

No appetite goes unsated,

Even the rooting mouths of the great Pacific Rainforests,

And taproots soak up nature's bone meal and spoor soup,

As the rains continue,

Pressure washing the dust of late summer

From needles and cones

And the giants sigh a long satisfied breath

And the rains continue,

Enveloping the world in a mist that cleanses and permeates

To the very heart of the land.

We wooded creatures purr

And circle soft beds in dark dens,

Welcoming the short winter days of silver shadows,

And sweet, dreamless sleep

Cats Fly a Sign

Every day on my way
To this place or that
I pass by a young man,
With his bike and his cats
In a box tied behind
Or belted in front, or
Sometimes he's standing,
Leash stretched to the max
While the cats sniff the gutters
Prowl bushes, or wax
Thoughtful,
As eyes yellow as moons
Watch traffic flow past.

And his cardboard sign begs
And blesses by turns
For mercy and cat food,
And my heart always yearns
To pack them all up
In my bright shiny car
And drive them to safety
Full bowls and warm bed.
But the light flips through changes

Like the thoughts in my head
And I drive on alone
Leaving so much unsaid,
Young man on the corner
Cold bowl
Empty bed.

Chapter 2
Singing the Blues

White Heat

So, you want me

When you're burning,

Slow fire raging

Between your legs.

You'll let me put it out

With my wet tongue.

Born to save, I'll crawl

For the pleasure of extinguishing

Your blaze.

Later, overcome by nausea

And contempt,

You kick me aside.

"Don't touch me there."

"Don't touch me."

"Don't touch."

"Don't!"

Next time, bitch,

You can burn in your fire,

You can writhe and you can moan,

But if I don't give it,

You ain't gonna get it.

I'll see to that,

And lips curling,

Slow smiling,

I'll watch you burn.

Timekeeper

Six-thirty-five P.M.

And a long, lonely evening

Looms before me,

Dark and empty,

An endless corridor

Of vaulted ceilings,

Where, here and there,

Trapped birds beat their wings

Against the smooth walls,

Sad calls,

Echoing my pain.

Ain't Nothin' Free

The Narrows Bridge in Tacoma
Fucked me up with her beauty.
Long limbed lovely
Stretching out before me,
A surprise on this slate-ugly day.
Rain stung my eyes
As I slid into her waiting arms.
I thought the click of the police camera
Was a wink from God,
And I sailed,
Mouth ajar with joy
Across ruffled amber waters.
Days later
The bill came in the mail,
Long since my ardor had cooled.

I didn't know she was a working girl

Flood Time

You want rain, girl,

I'll give you rain,

Torrents of clear dark water

Turned misty white in the dim light

Of our short winter days

Days of haze,

Can't see the mountains

Rain too thick,

Can't see the neighbors,

Windows too slick,

Can't see my lover

Eyes blind from crying,

Water, water, everywhere

Floods down my heart.

Oil Spill Tar Babies

We are three thousand miles away but
Can't escape the TV's flickering guilt trip.
The delicate sweep of spoonbill beak
Slipping down oil clotted tail feather.
There is no good end for this disaster.
Here, fog soaked and somewhat pristine,
Still wool-packed and damp with innocence,
My shuddering breath the only prevailing wind
In this rain drenched city
Where streetlights pool in puddles,
And reflect their golden globes off a low slung sky,
And my tear scarred eyes are sore with grieving.
This briny river of prayer
Is all I have to offer the Gulf of Mexico,
That sweet miracle of sands like sugar,
Warm waters swirling with life,
Now an overheated tar baby deathtrap,
Suffocating slowly under man's hubris
And nature's disinterested eye.

Friendless at Christmas

A foot of snow muffles

The parking lot outside

My bedroom window.

Christmas is cancelled.

I think I hate my life again,

Can't seem to get it right

Tears and shit leak through

The tattered seams of my existence.

I need to lose weight

But all I want to do is eat.

Am I so toxic that I repulse people

Or is that just how people are

Out here,

Independent, reclusive, closed off

And wary,

Like wolves going about their business.

Mercy Fuck

Yes, I want it,

But please don't do me any favors.

I feel your tongue,

A death rattle in my throat,

As pity replaces passion,

And your good deed

Tries to masquerade as love.

Foodstamp Blues

Yes, we are cared for by the State
Our food and medical needs addressed
as if by a caring entity.

But never believe that we fell willingly
into that dark abyss
Of poverty and pain,
Never believe it was a choice born of laziness
And low self esteem
Although loss of respect
Across the board
Is a price we pay for our daily bread.

Know only that we each fought,
Kicked and screamed,
Each in our own way we shunned the day
We entered the line.

Calendar Notes

May sucked

So I ripped it out.

Gulf got fucked

And my cat Marvin died

By my hand or the vet's

Death a commodity

Paid for in cash.

Glad to see May disappear

Sink below the oily black

Surface of Marvin's

Diseased and flakey coat.

Goodbye sweet boy.

Goodbye sad seas.

I give you back to Earth,

A soft bed of loam

Your new home.

Chapter 3
Family Affair

Birthright

Rachael & Ariel, moons of Ru, daughters,
Lamb of God sibling to Angel of Fire,
Darkness wed to light
Your poles shifting by turns one to the other
And back again,
Dizzying me with your quicksilver beauty.
Both strong willed and open-hearted
Walking the shadow places
With courage & compassion,
You are my twin goddesses,
My gift to this troubling world
This world's greatest gift to me.

And now, today,
I have looked into the azure eyes
Of my future generations,
Grandchild Zephyr, lies tucked,
fitting perfectly my curving arm
Neck stretching toward his mother,
Sensing separation, but calm,
Filled with bewildered wonder
At this bright busy place.

Plucked from the womb,
Quickly bundled,
And thrust into my arms,
He still has blood beneath his tiny nails,
Fresh and red,
A darker hue of the fiery ringlets
That crown his battered head.

He worked as hard as his mother
In this birthing,
We suspect there are tiny claw marks
Deep in her body
Where they still can be felt,
But not seen.
Scratchings at the door,
The door that would not open,
Could not open.
Perhaps he tried to tear though
Connective tissue that held like iron,
A family trait
Embedded in his mother's cells.
We'll never know.

But now we have seen the warrior in him,
Another family trait that runs strong in our blood,
At times both useful and problematic.

And I can see the lover,
Now in my arms,
Blond lashes so long, so lovely,
Brushing soft cheek as he nestles close.

Moving Day

My two small daughters are packing,
We are losing our home today.
Bright bundles of little girl's clothing
Lie scattered across the floor.
I am proud of their fearlessness
In the face of what is about to come
They chatter amiably
Discussing what to pack,
They seek opinions and confirmation with each other,
Wondering about the wisdom of their choices.
The house already looks deserted
And echoes with a sullen loneliness
That reverberates in my heart.
I wander out the kitchen door and I am struck dumb
By the beauty of a Spring-touched young forest,
Spreading out from our back yard,
Each tiny leaf an emerald
Making the very air sparkle.
I see garbage and litter on the ground,
But the trees are pristine,
I lift my arms and fly into them.

Fort Defiance – A Day at the Park

The lives of my ancestors depended

Upon building this fort,

Fort Defiance,

And making quick work of it.

"Mad" Anthony Wayne looked about,

Gorgonian head swiveling left to right,

Face greasy with the sweat of Manifest Destiny,

And blithely ordered the destruction

Of all Native American villages

And their crops

Within a 50-mile radius.

And then he began to build.

Slaves and military men carved massive planks

From the oldest and strongest oaks.

Mud the color of sweet potatoes

Was hauled up the steep riverbanks

By tail swatting donkeys,

Cementing his impregnable turrets

With rounded cubes of baked quagmire.
Mad Anthony built this westernmost outpost
In just one day longer
Than it took God to create the world.
His loyal men
built a sanctuary of steep walls and cannons,
And swore to protect the settlers
and their cherished children.
He kept them safe from the brutal British,
Who marched indomitable as red backed ants
Reticulating through green countryside,
And from the natives,
Stealthy, slipping through the mist,
Dark eyes seeking retribution
And dreaming massacre.
Of course, things eased up after the War of 1812,
And not long after William Henry Harrison
used the fort as a base
For his attacks on Tecumseh,
The Maumee River
became an industrious artery of free enterprise,
A winding skein of brown silty water

Finally connected

The settlers of this New World and those natives

Who survived our plagues of pox and guns.

Became, in fact,

A busy confluence of opportunity

For the small communities

Germinating along its muddy borders.

Now, two hundred years have passed

And a verdant, maple studded public park

Spreads its shady depth

Between a dusty baseball diamond

And the aquamarine swimming pool.

But the cannons, massive and grimy

With time and disuse,

Still aim their black maws across the river mists,

Military ghosts,

Shooting blanks on the 4th of July,

While modern children

Point plastic guns or sticks at each other,

And for a moment, the great massacres continue

Tumbling down through the minds of all.

House of Glass

I dream of houses without walls,
And I see the turning of universes between the
Wooden beams of my dream home,
And sometimes I find my life reflecting
This inclination toward transparency.
Suddenly, the walls I've known for years
Begin thinning to green lace and then disappear,
Flight calls and I know
I can soar through the icy stars,
Higher than I dare to think.
Only fear brings me back to earth,
Only fear holds me here.

I have an aunt
Who dulls her pain with cheap alcohol,
Purchased by the case,
And she piles these cases, high against the wall
Of her cabin in the woods.

She believes these cardboard and glass fortifications

Protect her from the ghosts

Of her shattered family,

While she drinks the cool amber

From endless brown bottles.

I mull this image over,

Buddha-mind looking to turn

Poison into medicine.

If it were me,

I would have cemented all those empty bottles

Lined up and layered into a strong wall,

Bottoms pointing toward the sun,

A house then, with green and brown circles of light

Shining through the walls

Like the golden eyes of an Egyptian cat goddess.

Blazing through the day,

Dimming only with sunset,

A house whose strong walls could never thin

To fern and vine with age and time

Never dissolving to transparency

Like the houses in my dreams.

Sailing

"I killed my father," the fat man said,
And though we knew he had long been dead
A guilty quiet descended,
Muffling the damp shush sherring
Of the weeping restless sea.
Sailing was one escape,
And we rode God's breath
All the way to the Cape,
But we couldn't leave the children,
Can never leave the children,
For they travel with you always,
The children you create,
And the child you are.
They scream and play, disturb your day
Whisper dark secrets into your curving ear,
High pitched echoes chatter your deepest fear,
We were all children once,
Some have died, some stayed around,
All waiting our turn in the
glittering ground.

Family Line

I was tired of sitting

At the head of the table,

Presiding over empty chairs

And abandoned toys.

The armoire against the far wall

My only companion,

Unadorned doors of mahogany,

Gleaming darkly and closed tight,

Secrets stored elegantly

In an otherwise impoverished room.

My Thursdays were special

Because of her,

But it was already seven

And she had not come.

Suffused with angst

I searched the crowded drawers

Looking for her number,

Any number,

I needed someone to come for me.

The lethargy of my illness
Was drawing me down,
I soon became heavy with inertia.
I went to the patio to get
A breath of air,
And I saw that my family
Was all gathered there,
A rose tinted portrait
Of three generations
Sitting serene in a line of lawn chairs,
A solid but cheerful
Line of lawn chairs.

Chapter 4
Matters of the Heart

Come Close My Love

The mist has dissipated
And you can see me now
Unguarded, standing alone,
An empty cup waiting to be filled
With the sweet summer wine
Of your company.
I long to know the fullness of you
Pouring into me.
Come near,
We have a delightful journey ahead of us.
Do not fear me, I am a gift given freely,
I am yours for the moment,
And you are mine,
Playmates and lovers
Partners and friends.
We belong together
And our time has come again.

Mirroring Phenomena

Sometimes the line between

Friend and lover

Thins to transparency

Shimmers

And

Dissolves

In the amber depths

Of my mind's eye

And I am lost in confusion

Looking to you

For the comfort of delineation

Only to meet myself again

in your gaze

High Tide

I love to feel your tides rising

Imperceptible at first,

Almost a wisp of my imagination,

A trick of the light,

A trick of the touch

Seabirds skimming lightly

Over the waves of my perceptions.

Half dreaming

My response is a slow

Sinuous awakening

Brought on by the gentle knowing

Of your fingertips

And the soft shudder of your breath

Against my neck.

Liquid fault lines

our bodies rise and shift

And settle again in perfect synchronicity

Exposing secret caves and tunnels

Underwater treasures

Velvet coral

Sweetened with delight.

I dive

And find a honey chambered nautilus

It opens to my tongue

And we are swept away,

Hearts pounding like the surf

Against the jagged shoreline

Of our desire.

Please Baby, Come

Please Baby,

Come.

Penetrate me with your love

And I will writhe

Exhaling a soft moan

And lift myself to you,

Give myself to you,

Twist myself slowly

To ease you into me

Even deeper

Ever deeper

Because that is where you belong,

That is how we belong

To each other,

Tremulous and erubescent

In the early dawn

Pulsating together

In measured beat

With the coming day.

Orange Is the Moon

Orange is the moon
I watch you under
As lavender clouds
Skitter past my drooping lids.
Am I dreaming this kaleidoscope
Of whites on silver
Or has night since fallen
And my shuddering hopes for reconciliation with it?

It is your guarded back I see
Walking away
Broad shoulders limned
By endless stars.
The great
Darkness swallowing all.

Nectar Eater

Girl, you had me blooming

Like a flower to the sun,

I ache from it

And from the memory.

Too quickly opened

And given just a taste,

Has made me crazy for you.

Now I know what hunger is.

Only time will tell,

And it stretches out before me

Vast as an ocean.

When will I be with you again?

Another Autumn

Sugar maples dance,

Leaves folding coyly

Over eyes rimmed in bark,

Flame tipped stanchions

Shuddering the wind

Across my sun-turned face,

Whisperings from the North

Goodbye the sun

And the ease of summer,

Comes the darkening grays of fall

To snow drenched winter

Melting into the sweet birthing

Of another fecund spring,

And begin again,

As the whirl of days, turn to seasons, turn to years,

Spanning lifetimes,

Spent apart.

Taurus Moon

It's a Taurus moon, and I'm thinking of you,

My polar opposite,

My one-time-fine-feathered-friend.

Is your hair long and grown in brown,

Tipped with gold?

Do you have remembrances of me,

And my crazy-colt of a daughter,

And the end of Summer?

My mother asks about you still,

I don't know what to say,

I've grown quiet on a lot of subjects.

My life ripped and roared through the Autumn,

But the silence of Winter was enough

To crack my eardrums,

Not exactly peaceful,

But a needed respite from the battles.

I pray for Spring,

Now that my house is insulated,

And my storm windows are finally up.

I seem, to have a knack for untimeliness this year.

They say, forgiveness is an art,

And I surely am no artist,

(Though I do remember creating some monsters)

But I miss our easy times together, do you ever?

I wish you well.

Over-Soul Love Song

Who better knows than I

Of what you are made, and how you are moved.

You may lie alone,

The mahogany pillars

Of your four poster bed

Soaring up to the ceiling

Sentinels in your dark night

Protecting you at each sacred corner

And covering you

With a canopy of lace,

Now turned to leaves,

Now turned to stars.

You may feel alone,

As you lie alone,

But this has never been so.

Always have I been here loving you

As you nestle in the curve of my arms

Warming yourself at the blazing hearth

Of my beating heart,

Enveloped in the sweetness of my breath.

Always will I be here for you

Loving you,

And praising you for your courage,

For you are luminous in your courage.

A spiritual warrior.

And I watch

Terrified and love struck,

As you seek to create and destroy yourself,

And create yourself again,

Burning through the layers of your essence

In an ecstasy of discovery,

Exultation

And

Lament.

Mercy (Dreamscape)

I've been institutionalized

And then cast out.

I'm healthier than most,

My body incandescently curvaceous

Beneath my hospital gown,

I'm still tuned-in

To a sweet raw current of sex

That purrs beneath my smile.

The hospital is in danger

And everyone must leave.

A silent group leads me to a young man

Who cannot be moved.

He is kept alive by the machines that surround him,

He cannot be detached or he will die.

He will never leave the building alive,

And he knows this,

We all know this.

I am to give him his last rites,

His last right,

The right of sex

And loving intimacy between strangers

Before we leave him

To die alone.

I am not fazed

Until I ask about his health.

The nurse mumbles, I can barely hear,

"He has AIDS," she says,

"And no lips.

We must paint them on every day."

I wonder how I can

Protect myself from this person,

And still be loving,

And still be intimate,

How to kiss lips already dead.

Passing the Night

It's midnight and snowing

And inside my mind,

I'm wandering lost

In a graveyard

Filled with dead love-affairs,

Digging here and there,

Sometimes furtively,

More often, resignedly,

Turning over the bones,

Looking for the truths

That outlasted the loves.

Shake, rattle and roll!

Can the remains of the past

Predict the future?

It's been said,

"A journey of one thousand miles,

Begins with a single step."

A lifetime of love could very well begin

With just one kiss,

And a little luck.

Well on our way,

We've already had one thousand kisses,

And more to come.

Roll over on me, sleeping beauty.

Let me feel the warm sweetness

Of your breath

Upon my neck.

Let me hold you for awhile,

Before we rise and separate.

You and your fiery lovings

Give me strength to greet the day.

Chapter 5
Summation

And Later

I felt cold-cocked

When we had finished talking…

Something cold

Forced deep within me.

Spreading numbness.

Still,

It was a release,

And I am grateful.

Any excuse to throw off

Another shackle.

The Nature of My Reality

The question radiates in my mind

Like a pebble striking water.

Where did I come from?

Where am I right now?

One foot stuck in the past,

The other reaching out for the numinous future,

There is an army of me,

Each persistent and skilled in her task,

Tendrils of memory flung back

Lassoing recipes and random facts

About car mileage, weather patterns

And how to care for cats.

I am so much and so many souls

Rolled up into one

Ever present bundle,

My own black hole,

In my own universe,

Everything comes to me,

To be swallowed and forged down

Into the heavy material world

That creates this present reality.

Nothing is ever wasted, nothing ever lost.

Conversations with Trees

The trees I've known have been singularly talkative

And often quite direct with their messages and warnings.

In fact,

That is how I ended up moving

To this cold northern place,

Where the sun shines only enough to feed the greenery,

And the air is crisp as a pruning knife

They started it.

They always start it.

Whispering enigmatically in the night,

Swirling their loose limbs about in the wind,

Low branches touching the earth,

Riding the rippling air

Of a Flamenco dancer's skirts.

The first time, years ago,

Living in a Southern state,

Desperate with loneliness and betrayal

I found myself driving a twisted mountain road,

With only a floating silver moon

To illuminate the winter dark,

When a full bellied cedar leaned out

And over me

And murmured, *"You   are   loved!"*

After that, each time I passed this tree,

My tires squealed as I held the curve,

And my heart bloomed warm and raw.

Another time, a brambled white oak

Reached across a broke down fence in Missouri,

Whispered, *"Come dance with me."*

Offered to help me end my life

Right then and there.

I knew that dance, we all do,

That dance of death.

I considered it.

It seemed so easy,

Just cross over into that silhouetted

Field of stars,

And leave my surprised body behind,

Slack-jawed with sudden death

I could gift her musician, the wind,

My very last breath.

Ironically,

This thought shocked my system so,

I ran into the house and slammed the door.

The last time they spoke to me,

The devastated oaks on the property,

Interrupted a Florida eclipse.

Their arms reached up and clawed the night

With branches stripped bare

By disease and blight.

While a hot wind shrilled,

"There is nothing more that you can do.

This land is dying and so will you!"

Then a swirling red dragon rose up, out of the mist

Covering the lopsided moon,

And I knew in my heart

The Agent Orange that was sprayed

By our neighbors next door,

Meant we needed to leave very soon.

It took ten months to pack my family,

Human, feline, canine, our treasures,

We moved to the Black Hills, my lover and I,

Being country women

We still craved the protection of the trees.

Now, we stare in dumbstruck amazement

At the towering firs of the Northwest,

And their fat,

Satisfied appearance,

Fecund as weeds.

I have even come to understand

How one could think

There were too many trees,

Crowding about the house,

Running long woody fingers

Irritatingly across one's window,

Scratching a chalkboard beat

To the wind-filled winter storms.

I watch and I listen,

Safe in their greenwood circle

I wait,

But they have not yet spoken to me,

They sit serene on their great haunches

Silent and watchful as cats.

The Wisdom of Crows

What alien spirit has taken over my tortured body
And warring mind,
Be-calmed me like the support and safety
This solid chair provides my trembling legs,
So my thoughts can slow their swirling circular flight,
Blackbirds settling
On a field of corn, raucous,
Feasting after the ferocious gathering,
Finally stilled into sunset
When they rise and disappear
With only the huff of wings in the darkness.

Content.
Could they be?
Can crow's eyes recognize the ecstatic frenzy
That precedes death?
Is this the final fullness?

Fare Thee Well

Blue eyes looking into brown

Goodbye again, farewell.

We part again,

To meet again,

And part again, somewhere.

The classic dance continues,

Of point and counterpoint,

As rhythmic and slow,

As all the years that flow,

Within,

And far beyond

Our separate lives.

Journeys End

Having finally arrived at journey's end

Burdened down with bags and kin,

I find you waiting

Loving still,

Your arms encircle me.

There is safety in a heartbeat

And a future in a glance.

Lay down

And let me comfort you,

Renounce our years of anger

And re-kindle our romance.

Reflections

I sit in my room

Alone

At the window

My mind

A blank slate

Gray as the sky

As an early spring rain

Sweeps in softly

Around me

And the blackened bare bones

Of trees

Long sleeping

Now burst forth

In a delicate profusion

Of laciness

Green,

As soft and as sweet

As a deep

Jungle dream.

Body of Work

My body is a bonsai tree,

Pruned

Grafted,

And shaped

By some unseen hand.

An artist with a sense of the Divine

And a taste for the voluptuous.

I am a highly evolved exotic,

And curvaceous

To my very bones.

Slender legs like reeds,

Keep tempo to their own rhythm

As I pass you in the streets,

Asymmetry harmonized

To mobile

Perfection.

The Need for Renewal

It didn't used to be
So difficult.

At 30, renewal was everywhere,
Women marched in the streets,
Taking Back the Night,
Taking back their bodies,
Taking back their souls,
Shave your head, pick up a sign,
Will yourself safe in the dark.

If only for a night,
We knew in that short
Emboldened parentheses of our daily lives,
That we were surrounded and lifted up
By hundreds of sisters,
The Army of Lovers that could not fail –
And didn't really fail,
But seemed to fade away,
As we acquired our own singular bravery,
We no longer needed each other,
Or thought we didn't, anyway.

And now, Daughters and Grand daughters
Spangled with metal piercings
and graffitied with tattoos,
Leather-clad and rainbow-haired
Go fearlessly into the streets.
They have no need to "come out"
They were born out.

The old paradigm has shifted,
And we, the once young, bright,
system crashing First Wave
Have sunk back into the homogeneous
warm sea of humanity
That brought us so alive at their age.

I know what I know,
And my tired back was a bridge
For this generation of women.
Might they not at least
give us credit for suffering the first blows as
We sought justice and equality
For our female-centric ways?

No, it is not the way of a revolution,
And besides,

Too much looking back
While traveling at this rate of speed
Can cause accidents.

But must I content myself
With living in the shadow
Of a lesbian nation I helped to create?
Must I allow myself to be cast
Into the pile of elders and crones
Whose stride is no longer strong,
Whose voices are no longer relevant?

I think not!
I am old,
But I have lived the truth of this revolution,
And I will not be silenced
By either apathy or disappointment.
I am tired,
But I still have the strength to always vote
"The Woman Card"
And bring this patriarchy to its knees.
I am no longer young,
Dew-kissed and lovely,
But I will continue to model a life
Of value and valor

As a Grandmother and Wisdom Keeper to
The next wave of empowered women,
And to the wave after that,
Until I finally slip beneath
The restless currents of human consciousness
To my own deep and satisfying final resting,
Until the next time, anyway.

Portrait by Ammah

Ru Otto is a poet, an artist and a frisky wheelchair diva who lives and works in Everett, WA. Her Sheltered Workshop is a working studio loft which she shares with two cats, thirteen fish, a frog, and her good friend, Janie Whited.

Ru has been writing for most of her life and has self-published three poetry chapbooks, a cookbook, and a children's book illustrated with her original watercolor paintings.

Contact info:

www.ruotto.com

ruotto46@msn.com

(360)349-2334   or (425)322-4815